SUMMARY:

JAB, JAB, JAB, RIGHT HOOK:

HOW TO TELL YOUR STORY IN A NOISY SOCIAL WORLD

ABBEY BEATHAN

Text Copyright © Abbey Beathan

All rights reserved. No part of this guide may be reproduced in any form without permission in writing from the publisher except in the case of brief quotations embodied in critical articles or reviews.

Legal & Disclaimer

Legal & Disclaimer

The information contained in this book is not designed to replace or take the place of any form of medicine or professional medical advice. The information in this book has been provided for educational and entertainment purposes only.

The information contained in this book has been compiled from sources deemed reliable, and it is accurate to the best of the Author's knowledge; however, the Author cannot guarantee its accuracy and validity and cannot be held liable for any errors or omissions. Changes are periodically made to this book. You must consult your doctor or get professional medical advice before using any of the suggested remedies, techniques, or information in this book. Images used in this book are not the same as of that of the actual book. This is a totally separate and different entity from that of the original book titled: "Jab, Jab, Jab, Right Hook"

Upon using the information contained in this book, you agree to hold harmless the Author from and against any damages, costs, and expenses, including any legal fees potentially resulting from the application of any of the information provided by this guide. This disclaimer applies to any damages or injury caused by the use and application, whether directly or indirectly, of any advice or information presented, whether for breach of contract, tort, negligence, personal injury, criminal intent, or under any other cause of action.

You agree to accept all risks of using the information presented inside this book. You need to consult a professional medical practitioner in order to ensure you are both able and healthy enough to participate in this program.

Table of Contents

The Book at a Glance vii

Introduction: Weigh in x

Round 1: The Setup 1

Round 2: The Characteristics of Quality Content and Compelling Stories 8

Round 3: Storytell on Facebook 13

Round 4: Listen Well on Twitter 18

Round 5: Glam It Up on Pinterest 24

Round 6: Create Art on Instagram 29

Round 7: Get Animated on Tumblr 32

Round 8: Opportunities in Emerging Networks 36

Round 9: Effort 39

Round 10: All Companies are Media Companies 42

Round 11: Conclusion 44

Round 12: Knockout 46

About the Author 48

Conclusion 49

Final Thoughts 52

Free Bonus #1: ....**Error! Bookmark not defined.**

Free Bonus #2: Free Book Preview of Summary: God: A Human History 54

The Book at a Glance 54

Introduction: In Our Image 57

The Book at a Glance

Gary Vaynerchuk likens doing business to boxing. The way a boxing match goes is closely similar to how businesses and consumers interact with each other. In the modern setting, of which social media marketing is an essential part, businesses jab their consumers by providing content that can entertain and inform. Depending on how the consumers respond, the business can then proceed to jab some more or go for a right hook, which is equated to the sale or closing of the deal. This engagement is what Gary believes to be the driving force between business-consumer interaction online and offline.

In this book, Gary intends to educate businesses and marketers, especially those with small businesses, in the way of social media marketing. With his expertise and experience from his own success and his clients' from VaynerMedia, he hopes to teach the reader how to succeed in getting their brand known by their target audience. In doing so, the reader will hopefully be able to capitalize and create results from effective offers and promotions done on social media platforms.

The first few chapters of this book delve on the current set-up of the world regarding use of mobile devices and social media networks. The progress of this evolution in media has happened in the same way in previous forms, particularly in print, radio, and television. He also iterates how the modern story-telling process works in marketing and how it was shaped to its current form by social media. Then, he enumerates valuable pointers on how to create valuable content that will be effective jabs to make your audience relate with your brand.

In the next part, he builds upon the characteristics of good content to provide insight on current best practices and effective marketing strategies on the most used social media platforms. Facebook, Twitter, Pinterest, Instagram, and Tumblr are tackled individually. For each of these platforms, the right kind of content is explained and some tips are given on how to create effective content native to the platform. He also explores the opportunities from some of the emerging social media networks.

Transitioning from the different social media platforms, he explains the importance of effort to achieve success in any area of life. He says that it is true that small businesses have a great disadvantage when it comes to resources. This greatly affects their capability to match the marketing efforts of bigger businesses. However, the disadvantage of being a small organization is an advantage in of itself as it enables such businesses to respond at a faster rate to their audience's needs, interests, and preferences. He reiterates that, depending on the quality of effort exerted, advantages such as capital, budget, and human resource can be overcome.

In the last part, he states that the requirements for success in the modern day are a lot more different than those in the past. This is mostly due to the technological and socio-cultural changes brought on by various modern advancements. More changes will occur and things will get more difficult. Nevertheless, in the scheme of things, this shouldn't be the problem if your mindset is that of constant learning and development to achieve and maintain the leading position. Having this mindset will equip you to always fight for that position and, in the process, you will constantly grow as a professional.

Introduction: Weigh in

Business, like boxing, has an aggressive, competitive, and fast-paced feel to it. This is no different in the world of social media marketing. Companies create big campaigns or promotions to create results that will give them advantage over their competition. Like the right hooks in boxing, they know that these events deliver sales and the return of investment for their business.

In the current setting, marketers create campaigns one after the other but they still fail in creating the results they are after. This failure is borne out of the assumption that, with a well-executed right hook, one can lessen or forego creating relationships with their customers. It would have worked in the age of television and digital media; however, social media has changed the dynamics of business-customer interaction.

Frequent and numerous promotional offers just do not work as much anymore as today's business; like boxing, it does not consist only of right hooks. Yes, often, only the right hook is seen as the punch that won the match. However, without the boxer (the business) delivering jabs (customer engagement), the delivery of the "right hook" would surely miss. Either the recipient of such promotions would ignore it or it will have no audience at all as it did not provide the requisite jabs for customer engagement.

The inspiration for this book came from the realization that Gary's success for Wine Library TV was a result of authentic and genuine content suited for YouTube. The author emphasized in his previous book, *The Thank You Economy*, and in his various speaking engagements that social media marketing should be done with the long-term in mind. There should be genuine and solid customer engagement as this will create active and real relationships with one's customers. However, as Gary realized, sales and return on investment cannot be achieved by only using customer engagement. There should be well-executed "right hooks", or campaigns and sales as well, to create the revenue that will spell success for the business.

In his first book, *Crush It!*, Gary taught the readers how to create great content and how to utilize content for the different platforms available at that time. Nevertheless, the changes in existing platforms and development of new ones have brought about the need to change past approaches to deliver successful right hooks in the current setting. With this book, all the knowledge from the first two books will be updated and combined to illustrate how to apply it in the current social media and digital environment.

Regardless of the type of company or organization you're in, your task is to tell the story of your organization, company, or brand to your customer. Especially now that what was done in print, radio, and television has a smaller audience as to what it used to before, and direct e-mails and banner ads are not as effective as before. The only option for the most effective marketing is through social media as this is where people spend most of their time now.

This book will set you up in how to tell your story on the most important social media platforms of the time. The storytelling formula will be taught to you so that your story will be effective delivering your message to your customers. An examination of some of the good, bad, and ugly stories done by different companies will be done to illustrate the common pitfalls in social media marketing. Once you've learn all this book can teach, you will be able to adapt to any new platforms in the future.

Jab, Jab, Jab, Right Hook is considered to be the last book in Gary Vaynerchuk's trilogy on the evolution of social media and of his career as a marketer and businessman. Although the world and the available platforms change, the secret to creating results remains the same. To attain brand awareness and profit through social media marketing, it requires the classic and everlasting values of hard work, passion, constant engagement, sincerity, long-term commitment, and clever and strategic storytelling.

Round 1: The Setup

The rules of marketing have changed compared to when people's only exposure to the internet and social media was through their desktop or laptop computers. With social media easily accessible literally almost always at the palm of our hands, it is bound to change how current and prospective customers interact with businesses, services, and brands. Because of this, businesses and marketers must adapt to these changes to create desirable results in the form of brand awareness, sales, and profit.

Where's Your Phone?

Almost everyone has a smartphone or tablet. Within four feet in a public setting, you could see almost everyone on their phones. The only time that this is not the case is in a nursing home, where senior aged individuals prefer tablets or iPads. When people are using these devices, they have a 50 percent chance that they are interacting on various social media platforms. With the fact that 75 percent of these users check their accounts at least once a day, it is a glaring truth that business cannot be done without social media marketing.

How Social Blended Digital

The traditional strategy of marketers is becoming ineffective. It won't do to simply divide marketing efforts into traditional, digital, and social. This is due to social media marketing playing a crucial role in the results garnered by a business' traditional and digital efforts. This new reality was and is being experienced by businesses that invested into campaigns and got lackluster results due to a lack of social media effort. However, for those who had the wisdom to properly do these three together, the campaigns for each platform were able to create massive conversions and brand awareness.

The current state of marketing is not surprising, as every new form of media has always taken the audience of the one that came before it and created changes on how marketing practices are done. The rate at how fast one media is adapted by the general audience becomes faster from the introduction of one form to a new one. To illustrate, it took 40 years for almost everyone in America to own a radio, while television and social media only took 13 years and a year and a half, respectively. With the easy and instant access people have with the reigning form of media, social media, the concept of an audience's undivided attention is a thing of the past, as people are constantly multi-tasking - consuming and chattering on social media while doing their day-to-day tasks.

Unfortunately, at the cost of diminishing returns, some businesses, entrepreneurs, and marketers do not seem to understand the new rules of marketing. Although they have created accounts to be present on Facebook and Twitter, their efforts seem empty, as they have stayed within the confines of these platforms. They do not understand that social media has changed the game of marketing and that every marketing campaign in any one form of media should synergize with social media to create customer engagement.

Furthermore, with the current consumer spending at least ten percent of their day on mobile, businesses have no right to expect their business to garner remarkable results from social media marketing if it is only one percent of their advertising budget. Businesses cannot expect consumers to like their content if their social media content was just repurposed from one platform to the next. It would be like using radio marketing content for television marketing and being surprised that consumers did not care whatever it had to say. Businesses and marketers must properly use social media if they want to create results from their social media marketing efforts.

This book will show you the ropes on how to create relevant and value-driven content that will catch the consumer's attention and compel them to share, which results in the sales and brand-awareness marketers are going for. Regardless of how big or small your business is, the rules are the same: it matters when, how, and where the story is told.

How Storytelling is Like Boxing

Before the advent of social media, marketing campaigns came in the form of one-sided boxing matches wherein businesses and marketers threw fast and frequent right hooks. It worked, as the consumer had no choice but to accept what was essentially the practice of the time. Media had no input from the side of the consumer and marketing campaigns involved only grabbing their attention.

With the introduction of social media, the consumer was given a voice and a capability to dictate how these interactions would go. Jabs, or little pieces of content, that capture interest and attention for engagement, have become a requirement, as the former practice of fast and frequent right hooks just did not work anymore. Without these jabs, the right hooks, or the call to actions or promotions, did not have the conversions it used to garner in the age of traditional and digital media. In addition to this, it changed the game completely as periodic marketing campaigns became a thing of the past and the daily campaign has become a necessity.

Most businesses and marketers, even those who got into social media marketing from the very start, are still being slow in adapting to new social media platforms. They see a new one and only look at it for a few minutes wherein they would see the expected low quality content of these platforms while in their infancy. With this brief experience, businesses write it off as a fad or deem as not worth the risk for high likelihood of failure. Then, after a few months to a year, they would go back into the platform, see the successes of the few brave ones who dared to take the risk, and adapt the formerly new platform. However, at this point, they are playing catch up and have already missed the chance of being seen as a pioneering brand in the platform.

Open-minded marketers and businesses must see these new platforms in the context they are meant to be used and come up with ways to capitalize it from the very start. They must realize that results can only be achieved with the long-term in mind. If they do it right, they are likely to reap the rewards of being touted as pioneers in strategy by traditional and digital media. With this media attention, their chances increase in attracting young talented individuals and they will also create increased awareness for their brand from such media coverage. Of course, marketers must be aware that success is not assured in these platforms. This is why they have to play the long game while learning and adapting along the way.

Marketers and businesses must put the reality of the market and the audience's media habit above their own and the organization's principles and preferences. They must approach emerging technology and platforms with a positive and long-term outlook, and a respect for the context of each social media platform.

To achieve success in marketing, they must act now on new trends and platforms with aggressive offense and not with risk-averse defense. Refusing to adapt to present day practices and to your audience's preferences will get your business out-of-touch and make engagement difficult between you and your customers. It will even be worse for your business if your competitor is more forward-thinking than you.

The Sweet Science

The fixed storytelling blueprint does not exist. The feedback to what you do can be immediately seen on the various social media platforms through hearts, shares, comments, likes, re-pins, and re-blogs. You should go beyond experimentation and adapt to what your results indicate. From here, you will get the blueprint that works for your brand. However, remember that this blueprint is not permanent and, just like any boxer, you will have to change your strategy.

As each platform is unique, a blueprint will have to be adapted according to the context of how content is consumed in it. The native language of these platforms must be utilized by the small and frequent content you create to establish connection with your audience. Of course, the right hook should be effective in the manner that is simple, easily understood, created for mobile and digital devices, and, like the jabs, should respect the platform's context for content.

Round 2: The Characteristics of Quality Content and Compelling Stories

For effective content, social media requires it to be noticed by a platform's users. In their bid to be noticed, marketers and businesses will constantly post a steady stream of new content in their social networks. This content often lacks the imagination and creativity to spur the interest of social media users. For social media users, these types of posts are just wastes of space and, as a result, will just be ignored. Here are the rules of great content that have created great success for Gary Vaynerchuk's business and clients:

Native

Content should be delivered in the format that is appropriate for the given social media platform. If it is not, it will most likely be ignored by your audience, as it will seem out of place and limited by the platform's context. It must be exactly like the content being posted by other users of the social media platform. It tells a story like it was told by a human being while catching the interest of the audience.

Creating content native to the platform is not new. The first television commercials were just in the form of a voice saying that a program was presented by some brand, product, or company. These obviously did not work – it did not catch the interest of the viewers. This changed when these advertisements started coming in the form of short stories with relatable characters.

From a disembodied voice to stories with characters, the advertisers simply adapted their advertisements to be in a similar form that the audience sought from a television. This form consists of a story and characters. In social media, you will be doing the same as what these television advertisers did to create effective content. You will create content that has the same form as what people are looking for in a given platform.

Does not intrude

Although some traditional and digital ads can be entertaining, they still intrude into the audience's media experience. Effective social media marketing cannot act like its predecessors, as people do not have the patience for it anymore. If marketers and businesses want to engage with their audience during their time on social media, their advertisements should be the actual source of their entertainment. They should also replicate the experience people are trying to seek from their platforms so that their content does not break or distract the audience from their experience.

It does not (frequently) make demands

Your content should be valuable to your audience. Content is valuable when it, at least, provides one of the following: genuine interaction with the audience, helpful information and interesting trivia, and entertainment as a means for them to escape. With it, you're not asking for a commitment or a purchase from your consumer or audience. You're just sharing a funny, informative, or heartwarming moment together that creates good will and connection with your audience. When your brand gives its sales pitch, they will feel like you're that friend who has given so much that they would just think it's rude to refuse.

Leverages popular culture

The content you generate has one purpose: to create a connection with your audience. One of the most effective ways to create this connection is by showing that you understand them. It could be having the same interests in music, being on top of the latest news of celebrities of their generation, and understanding issues that matter to them. With not only the young generation consuming their media from their mobile devices, you can reach different generations by reaching out to their interests and preferences and establish a relationship with them.

Micro

You have to rethink your perception of content. It should be micro. It should be the tiny and unique commentary, humor, information, and inspiration from the day-to-day. As a marketer in the age of social media, your concerns do not only include the sales of your product and your audience's awareness of your brand but, also, includes the production of constant, timely, frequent, and unique micro-content. Social media is not just a back-up for your other efforts but it is a main area in marketing and creating brand awareness for your business.

Consistent and self-aware

While your micro-content varies from your every post and platform you use, it should still be consistent with the identity of your business or brand. The message your brand conveys should be consistent on the micro-content produced in the different platforms. The message and the form of the micro-content are just like the different outfits a person wears according to the occasion. It is a means your brand adapts to become noticed and to remain relevant for your audience.

Round 3: Storytell on Facebook

One out of every five page viewed in the U.S. is on Facebook. It is the biggest social network and has driven the culture in the age of social media. This is where people go to catch up, connect, and socialize with people they know and care about. In the process of this connection and socialization, they find out what their acquaintances prefer and do, and they respond accordingly by liking, sharing, and commenting on these content.

Facebook ranks the content in its sphere through their algorithm EdgeRank. It analyzes how people responded to content posted by social and business users alike. Their ranking varies from time to time but it is mostly based on the number of shares, likes, and/or comments.

Because of this algorithm, marketers must create content that will cause their targeted audience to click like or share and make them engage through comments. Of course, your content must stay fresh for your audience so it is a must to constantly reinvent daily content and to be in touch with your audience's interests and preferences.

Doing Micro-Content in Facebook

Due to how the algorithm works, you must first get your audience to like the content you create. This is done because, when you put out that right hook, you want a lot of people to see it. Micro-content is the only way to show Facebook and its users that people care about the content you produce. Without micro-content that people find interesting and interacted with, only a small portion of your audience will get to see the right hook, which could be in the form of a promo, offer, or any other call to action.

Targeted Content

You can target your content to a select segment of your audience. This can make micro-content more effective while being the difference for a call to action's success. Targeted content can increase the chances of people interacting with your micro-content through engagement or call to actions through click-through, which will improve your EdgeRank numbers while reducing indifferent individuals from viewing it.

Of course, by using this approach, you will have to spend to get Facebook to target your intended audience. However, compared to television and print advertising, it is significantly cheaper as, provided it is quality content, your audience will increase its reach through likes, comments, or shares. With social media content meant to be shared, your spending for each targeted view is worth more than how much you paid.

Although the right side advertisement views are decreasing due to increased mobile use, Facebook adapted its methods of sharing targeted content to mobile. This approach does not intrude with the experience of your audience and, with the right content, blends seamlessly with the content of social users. Marketers who don't know any better think of this as a bad way to advertise. Nevertheless, by blending in, your audience won't resent you for interrupting their social media experience.

Sponsored Stories

This is one of the ways Facebook lets businesses show targeted content on their users' feed. How it sets itself apart from other targeted content is it rewards interesting and good content by letting audience see it more. If it's uninteresting and spam-like according to user response, the business will have a very limited reach with said content.

It is done this way as Facebook benefits if the consumer has a good and uninterrupted experience from using their platform. By giving more exposure and a better deal to good sponsored content, businesses and marketers must adapt to get their content viewed by their targeted audience.

Through sponsored stories, a business' page can expose their content to more users than their page currently has. If the content is so good that it causes those who see it to comment, like, or share it, this sends out a message to Facebook that people like it. The platform will give more exposure of content from this page so future posts will get more exposure. All of the additional views are free, as they are simply a result of your business page getting a higher number in EdgeRank. If quality content is continuously published, it will snowball into the future with just a single paid story.

Make Quality Sponsored Content to Save Money

The sponsored story won't let advertisers spend more than the actual worth of the content. If the targeted audience likes a sponsored content, Facebook prioritizes it over a competition's sponsored story. They will also give the content's marketer lower rates for future content. When engagement with this content dies down, it will eventually be pushed out of people's feed by newer and more engaging content. Of course, marketers can choose to keep paying to retain it in their audience's feed. Facebook does this to preserve user experience, which makes the high engagement level of your sponsored content in their best interest. By making good sponsored content, you're not only increasing the chances of good audience engagement but you're also paying less for it and your future content.

Checklist of a Good Facebook Micro-Content

Is the text condensed?

Is the photo high quality or striking?

Is there a visible logo?

Is it the right format?

Is it entertaining, provocative, or surprising?

Is it interesting for anyone?

Is this too much for the person viewing this content?

Round 4: Listen Well on Twitter

Twitter employs rapid conversations and idea exchanges as its native content. To achieve success in this platform, you have to add context that is unique to your brand and valuable to Twitter's audience. It is not enough to simply put out the links of your website, review, blog, or article. You have to interpret, remix, and spin the information you're linking to into a style that is uniquely your own. This is why you can use links from websites other than your own, as long as this information has value and you can spin it in a way that resonates with your brand and your audience.

Expand Your Universe

The short statements that you create are the way for your brand to establish a voice and position on Twitter. Through these statements, you are providing micro-content that can help your audience establish an identity for your brand. Unlike Facebook, Instagram, and Tumblr, the content, except for specifically set to private, are available for public viewing.

You can access and join conversations that arise from a stranger's tweet. Unlike in other platforms, joining in on these conversations is welcomed and accepted as the norm.

Furthermore, if your audience knows you're on Twitter, they can grab your brand's attention, which you can capitalize to increase customer engagement and, if it is a negative feedback, to mitigate a bad customer experience.

With Twitter, you can engage directly with your customers without looking like an intruding individual. You can look for topics being talked about in the platform related to your brand or business and add value to these conversations with your own context, humor, or perspective. Through these engagements, your brand becomes human and people can relate to it more.

Trendjacking

Twitter can track the trends arising from the hashtags used by its users. You can monitor trends arising from a national, regional, and worldwide level. You can use these trends to create micro-content in the form of tailored content made by you to create interest on your offer among those who have no idea about your brand. Alternatively, if you prefer to not create your own content, you can ride on other's content by providing your own context to these stories.

Of course, you have to also set some standards to how you're going to do about this. The poorest way to go about this is through re-tweets. There is no context added and your followers and other Twitter users will most often see it as lazy. Moreover, it does not really set you apart from other brands as a lot of brands do it.

Promoted Tweets

Using trending hashtags will require only the time to see how you can create your context out of it. Nevertheless, you can also get a promoted tweet riding on a hashtag. Through clever use of the right hashtag, you can create an impression for a small investment. With people spending most of their time on mobile phones, a simple and inexpensive placement of an ad can be a more effective exposure than a pricey television advertisement.

Using Trends to Create Call to Actions

Trending topics can be anything that catches the fancy of Twitter users. It could be names, current events, memes, or any word or phrase that went viral. These can be easily utilized to create valuable content or stories that can catch the interest of your followers. Since these trending hashtags are clicked by a lot of people, someone will most likely see your spin on the hashtag, like it, and check out your profile page to see more of your content. Once there, this new person can see more of your story from your frequent jabs and few right hooks. If they like what they see, they will follow you and you will get a probable customer in the future.

Your future customer does not even have to be the one who followed you. Your new follower could re-tweet your current or future content and one of their followers sees it and piques their interest. It could be a jab that causes them to follow or it could be a right hook that their follower is interested in. Either way, you would gain something out of the connection you just gained.

As long as you get creative and respond fast, you stand to gain by using these trends. You do not have to limit yourself with what's trending on Twitter, as you can use events or names trending on Google. Listen to what's trending and apply your own take on it. Regardless if what you put out is a jab or a right hook, it shows your followers and other users that you're a brand that pays attention. This can go a long way in acquiring new customers and gaining new followers.

Choosing Hashtags

You shouldn't just write as much hashtags as you can pack on a sentence. It will look unnatural for your brand and not native for the social media platform. You also cannot adopt a "cool" vocabulary in spinning these hashtags if your tone is naturally thoughtful or serious. You would just be pretending someone you're not but, on the other hand, your tone cannot be too serious all the time. Your voice should be organic and as human as it can be.

This does not excuse your brand to be not updated with the current trend. People won't be able to relate to you if you're talking in a way that they're not familiar with. In addition, you won't be able to join their conversations if you're not able to relate to them. Yes, it's true that it will take effort to keep up with popular culture. However, the work bears more fruit for your bottom line than simply sitting and waiting for your customers to notice you.

This is where small businesses excel. Since they do not have a PR or legal department to tell them what to do and not to do, they can be flexible and quick in responding to what's trending on the platform. They have more freedom in conveying their thoughts, humor, and commentary. This makes them much more human, which people will naturally find more engaging.

Keep on the lookout for opportunities of engagement. By spinning compelling content from people's conversations and information, you can nudge people who have no idea about your brand that they have something in common with you. This can be the opening for a conversation that can help your business win new clients or followers. Since you do not have to create your own content to do this, your brand can have an easier time doing this frequently in the day. All you have to do is stay updated with popular culture, get to know your audience, and respond in a way that is genuine with your identity.

Checklist for Good Twitter Content

Is it straight to the point?

Is the hashtag memorable and unique?

Is the attached image of high quality?

Does it sound authentic? Will it resonate with Twitter's audience?

Round 5: Glam It Up on Pinterest

Women comprise five out of six users in Pinterest. This makes it a non-negotiable social media platform when your products are sold to women in at least one way. With creative and evocative use of images, you can execute jabs and right hooks that can help your brand sell its products or services.

Pinterest was created with the intention of serving as a user's online collection of images that they love or pique their inspiration. Images consisted of food styling and recipes, fashion looks, and home decoration and renovation ideas. Then, when users exploded to almost 50 million people, the scope of the images being circulated exploded as well. Images of people's different hobbies and interests expanded the collection of images in the platform.

However, despite the potential for marketing and the platform's popularity, businesses were not taking advantage of Pinterest. It might be the fear that businesses might be sued for using images of other businesses. However, with how Pinterest functions as simply a network of people admiring the subject of images, there is no chance that a business will sue another for pinning an image or link because they like it.

Why Pinterest is Popular

Pinterest became popular because it made it easy for people to collect their ideas and research in one place, known as "pinboards". Moreover, it is similar to how we display art, items, or photos in our locker, work space, car bumper, or homes, that serve as a statement of our identity or goals. Because of this, Pinterest has been able to satisfy two powerful drivers of human nature – aspiration and acquisition.

How can businesses benefit from it? Surveys and studies have confirmed that users use it as their material and emotional check lists. Researchers found that Pinterest users are more likely to purchase something they see on the platform by 79 percent than on Facebook. It has been recorded to produce four times more revenue-per-click than Twitter. Businesses that learned the ropes and got into it have increased their revenue by 60 percent.

Yes, there will be businesses that will be a natural fit for Pinterest. However, through creativity, you can find various ways for your product or service to gain exposure on it. Even if your product is limited for such a platform, you can take a certain aspect of your product that can be brought to light with Pinterest.

How to Pin

Any image that you intend to use for interest must be visually compelling. It should invite people to click for a closer look. If your images cannot do so, users won't be able to know your story and your brand won't be able to penetrate their lives. This standard must be satisfied for the content you create and the content you re-pin from other boards.

For images of your products, indicating the price has been seen to increase the likes and click-through by 36 percent. You should also link these images to your website so you can conveniently convert a click into a customer. You can also increase engagement and brand awareness by providing valuable context and content to the product you're selling. This could provide quality content on how users can use your product or other context spins that can be applied. Through the context you create, you show users that you sympathize with their experience and prove that your product has a role in their life. With your clever context, you encourage users to re-pin your content, which increases the exposure of your content to other users and the chances of clicks to your board. Then, with your image link, you can lead them to your website where you can execute your call-to-action.

Building a Community for Your Brand

Comments on Pinterest are rarely used. You can easily take advantage of this by being the rare few who provides their own context on other people's content. You can seek pins that align with your interests and talk with the people who posted them. You can express your interest with your comment and start a conversation from there. These engagements can make people interested in you and cause them to click your name. By clicking your name, they'll see your boards and browse through them, making it likely for them to pin some of your content.

Another way to engage with users is by making your titles and captions provocative. Create titles and captions that will encourage those viewing your images to comment. From there, you can start the conversation and build a relationship. By doing these two things, you are essentially building your community, users who know you, on Pinterest.

Keep to the Rules

The rules of doing business in the real world are the same on how to do business on Pinterest. You have to convey a pleasant and caring disposition to the general audience and your target audience. You have to display your products in a way that pleases the eyes and evokes their curiosity. You are expected to be truthful and generous with your area of expertise. Take advantage of every moment that you can tell your story about your brand and its values. If by any chance you can't provide what they're looking for, help by pointing them in the direction of someone who can. Once you've done two or more what was said, you will have established a connection with them and this is when you will give them your call to action.

Checklist for Good Pinterest Content

Does the image feed the consumer's dream?

Do my boards have clever and creative titles?

Have I appropriately indicated the price of my wares?

Do my images have a hyperlink?

Could the pin act as an ad and a photo for an article in a top-flight magazine?

Can the image be easily categorized by users on their Pinterest boards?

Round 6: Create Art on Instagram

Like Pinterest, Instagram is centered on the concept of sharing visual content in a social network. It is designed to share mobile photographs and it does it very well. The only downside for a marketer is you cannot embed hyperlinks to your images. This can make it more difficult to direct your audience to your product or service page.

Even with its limitation as an image-sharing platform, businesses should not ignore the potential of Instagram for marketing their brand. The reasons for purchasing ad pages on magazines are the same reasons why you should utilize Instagram for your business. Unlike magazines, Instagram offers interaction in the comments, a sharing and distribution element, and tagging for increased exposure and awareness. With the number of active users in it, businesses have no reason to ignore Instagram's potential if they are willing to pay for advertisement on magazines.

Just keep in mind that you still have to follow the concept of frequent micro-content and infrequent call-to-actions. Frequently inserting links in your description or comments can look like spam for the users and your followers. Choose the right image and the right moment for inserting that link for your call to action.

Tips for Creating Successful Instagram Content

Make it native. People use Instagram for the quality images available in the platform. They don't scroll through the images to look for stock photos and advertisements. Users expect artistic, original content. Use the platform for the authentic expression of your brand's identity.

Make content with the younger generation in mind. The young generation consists of a majority of Instagram users. Create content that will resonate with their interests, humor, and language.

Maximize hashtags. There's no limit in the number and manner you use hashtags on Instagram. You don't have to limit its use to the content, context, and subject of your image. There's nothing stopping you from inserting hashtags next to each other so that it makes the arrangement incoherent. With these hashtags, users who click on similar ones from other images will see a page full of images with said hashtag.

Increase chances for getting into the Explore page. Instagram rewards the photos that users find the most evocative and artistic by placing them on the Explore page. Create great content that will cause your users and hashtag browsers to like it. The number of likes is an important criterion for getting into the Explore page. Getting into this page will increase your chances of new followers, which will translate to increased brand awareness.

Checklist for Good Instagram Content

Is the image artistic? Is it "indie" enough?

Have you included enough hashtags to describe your photo?

Does the story appeal to the young generation?

Round 7: Get Animated on Tumblr

Tumblr has a young and artsy user base consisting primarily of women. It has an easy-to-use and minimalist format that sets it apart from the common text-heavy websites. It is perfect for those intending to share their thoughts and ideas but would rather not write. With this platform, you are getting a blog, media, and social network platform rolled into one.

Excellent Branding Potential

What makes Tumblr an excellent branding platform is that it lets users complete customization capability on their pages. You can choose to use Tumblr-designed themes right out of the box, tweak these themes to your preferences, or create a look created just for your page. This capability lets you have the look that completely reflects your brand's identity and values.

What Makes It Unique

Tumblr does not use social connections to provide its user the content they can scroll through on their feeds. It connects people based on their interests. This gives you an opportunity to reach an audience completely unaware of your brand. With the right content, you can get your content on their feed.

Aside from this, Tumblr is the only social network that lets you post Graphics Interchange Format images, or GIFs. If you've seen those looping images, those are GIFs. These have been adopted as live emoticons to convey their expressions online. You might think that there's no way people would engage with low quality moving pictures. However, research says otherwise, as they found out that GIFs will get three times more likes than a high quality photo. By using these images, you can give your content some flair that only GIFs can convey online.

Why it's a Great Platform for Micro-Content

Although it is more of a publishing platform, Tumblr users still consume its content at an incredible rate. Like Facebook, Twitter, and Instagram, users can continuously scroll through their endless stream of content. This provides you with a great opportunity to produce micro-content that will tell your brand's story and create impressions upon your audience.

However, your content should be of the level that its users would like. Tumblr's audience is more artsy than the other social networks. You have to figure out and study the platform and what the users are looking for. By knowing what they are looking for and the audience, you can provide micro-content that is native to the platform and that can stop them from their endless scrolling.

Like Twitter, you can use other people's content and apply your own spin to it. If done right, it can make your posts more relatable and appreciated because of the authentic context you applied. Moreover, with hashtags, you can make your content easier to find.

Creating call-to-actions is possible but caution and discreetness is recommended. Focus on micro-content to tell your story and create your brand identity. When you've got a good following and good reception on your content, users will be comfortable to let you make your offer to them. A link to your website or to your retail site is enough and, based on your content quality, your audience might even be encouraged to make a purchase.

Checklist for Good Tumblr Content

Does the customization for the brand's page reflect its identity?

Does the post contain a cool GIF?

Does the context respect what the Tumblr community wants from their content?

Round 8: Opportunities in Emerging Networks

New or under-utilized platforms provide limited or no opportunities for call to actions. However, it never hurts to check how it can influence your audience or how it can provide valuable micro-content to its small audience. Facebook and Twitter started just the same way of having little potential for right hooks. However, those who got started early on said platforms had a distinct advantage as they have already a following before their competitors.

LinkedIn

LinkedIn is very similar to Facebook. If Facebook is concerned with socializing and entertaining through content, LinkedIn is where you create connections and content to network professionally and get deals done. Since it is a business-oriented site, there is an expectation that things are done to get a deal, sale, or hiring done.

It is a good platform for providing more lengthy content that can let businesses and individuals show their expertise. It gives business-to-business marketers a place to network, which Facebook does not provide. Since users will expect a professional setting, you can be less flashy but, at the same time, show that you're indispensable. The native content you produce must be free of slang but still have a breath of fresh air to stand out in a serious environment.

Google+

There's just not enough interest in this platform to be considered a viable platform for marketing. In its current state, Facebook already offers what Google+ provides. The only reason why it seems to have a lot of users is the sign-up requirement to access Google's other products.

Provided that Google Glass takes off and Google chooses to close it from other applications, it can rival Facebook for usage time and user numbers. It has the possibility of replacing mobile phones as the Glass provides a hands-free replacement. This can cause users to spend more time in their dormant accounts. With it being similar to Facebook, businesses do not have to relearn and can simply adapt their Facebook strategy into it.

Vine

Vine restricts users to only six seconds worth of video content. This restriction can limit the creativity but it can also force creators to adapt new ways to tell their stories. The six-second limit can encourage users to watch more videos than how much they normally would on YouTube.

The six second limit can increase the chances of users watching a marketer's video. With the right creativity and editing technique, marketers can tell their story that will catch attention and keep users coming back for more. Unfortunately, this platform is still new for it to have proven methods for marketing and creating awareness for a brand.

Snapchat

On Snapchat, users can send or broadcast photos and videos to their followers. Although known for being a sexting platform, it offers a lot of potential in sharing content that won't be kept for analysis or quality reasons. It is great for offering content that can offer a quick laugh, amusement, or information. With the right content, businesses can become the choice source for users to get their quick fix of content. Since the video will disappear in a few seconds, your audience will have more incentive to immediately watch it.

Round 9: Effort

In any area of life, effort makes us all equals. It doesn't matter if the business you're competing with has more capital than you have. It doesn't matter that they have a more expensive marketing budget than you do. It doesn't matter that they have a hundred individuals on their payroll while you're just a one-man operation. What matters in your pursuit of success is the amount of effort you put in your work.

Social media gave the small guy an advantage – it allowed them to compete on an even playing field with the corporate giants in the industry. As long as they were nimble, creative, and determined enough, they had an advantage on reaching the consumers first. However, big businesses adapted and invested in social media marketing. It took away the small guy's advantage.

However, taking away the edge small businesses had does not mean that they do not have a chance of taking on the big businesses. Small businesses can still win through their effort. The money invested into marketing efforts does not affect how much sincerity, heart, and effort goes into conversations with one's customers. Although you're limited by how many you have engaging with customers, you still have complete control with the things that matter - how well you talk with your customers and build your community of followers.

If you create good quality micro-content and call-to-actions, the audience will comment. Creative and sincere responses with these comments can create conversations that can enrich your relationship with your audience. If you have to, tag them in your comments to make sure they see that you acknowledged and replied to their comment. Clear up details regarding your offers and be helpful and accommodating with their questions or inquiries.

Moreover, in these conversations, be your authentic charming, funny, caring, and entertaining self. This will create the real connection and loyalty from your audience for you because they see how much you care for them as an individual and as a customer. This kind of caring from a business happens so rarely that it will set you apart from your competition, regardless of how big or well known they are in the industry.

In social media marketing, the fight goes on for the whole year and it will go on for successive years after that. Brands, which have been established through their marketer's consistent and skillful micro-content and call to actions, do not have to engage quite as much as the newcomer or the brand with a damaged reputation. Nevertheless, this is not always the case. Constant quality engagement is still an edge that can help your business to take over the lead and keep it there. Resting and getting lazy with your efforts will not do anything good for your business except to have the second-best knock you out of the lead.

Round 10: All Companies are Media Companies

From all the previous chapters, it has been emphasized that the key to successful social media marketing is micro-content. It does great in social media for it is easily consumed by its audience. However, this does not mean that it has less of an effect than media of greater length. In fact, long-form content still has significant merits in marketing in the form of magazine articles, YouTube videos, TV shows, books, and movies.

It is an area companies have taken advantage of in the past. Michelin Tires started publishing rural tour guidebooks in 1900 to increase the demand and usage for cars and tires. Guinness Breweries created in 1951 the Guinness Book of World Records to emphasize their brand in conversations in pubs. This can still be a development today as Nike can get into sports programming, and Amtrak, into travel publications. As long as these brands are transparent of their marketing efforts, people will appreciate it and the brand will be able to get better promotion.

This can give companies a better bottom line as they have an evergreen means of marketing their brand. Through these efforts, they are publishing content constantly that is actually valuable for their audience. They own it, which helps them cut costs for renting media for advertisements, and the brands gain invaluable brand recognition and reach from it.

Obviously, some people, especially the older individuals, will be skeptical about companies adapting a more active media approach. However, with how the future is shaping, there are those who recognize the need and the benefits of it. With the need for transparent and authentic means of marketing, these approaches that add value to their audience are increasingly gaining ground as a means for improved and more practical brand promotion.

Round 11: Conclusion

Figuring out how to unleash the full potential of a social media platform will take a lot of time and effort. With seven social media platforms being widely used, it can be a daunting task for a business tasked with keeping profits up. Nevertheless, being familiar with these platforms will give you and your business great returns in the immediate and eventual future.

It is true that changes unpredictably happen in these platforms. However, businesses and the users are slower to adapt to these changes. This gives you an edge ahead of your competition if you choose to actually invest in understanding how these platforms work. With almost no one attempting to learn how to properly use Google Analytics, it shows how much marketers are actually putting their time into understanding this crucial factor in social media marketing. By understanding how it works, you have already put yourself in the lead of almost everyone doing social media marketing.

If you put in the time and effort to understand the platforms and apply what you've learned in this book, you and your business can dominate the industry. There will be changes to the algorithms used by these social media platforms.

However, if you do what you did before to truly understand said platforms, you will immediately be ahead and have your competitors playing catch up.

They will eventually catch up as they understand it eventually, but you have a few months to a few years of being ahead of the pack wherein you're more effective than them. If you've made being on the lead your standard, there shouldn't be any difference to what happens as you will eventually be on the lead the next time changes are made.

Round 12: Knockout

The modern world changes from one second to the next and from one day to the other. This made the skill sets required for one to be a successful entrepreneur, celebrity, or marketer completely different from the skill set required for one to be successful ten years ago. It does not matter that these skill sets were relevant in the previous decades. The modern world has completely made it obsolete.

This is because marketing has become a living element that keeps getting harder and harder as progress is made. Nevertheless, there's no time to gripe about the intricacies of this industry in the modern world. The responsibility of today's marketers is to adjust to these realities and keep up to the changes, as it has no intention of slowing down.

At the time of this writing, video content has been implemented on Instagram. However, there will be more technological and platform advancements in the future that will make your job as a marketer both refreshing and difficult. There will be changes incorporated in these that will require you to reevaluate how much micro-content to produce before putting out the offer to your audience.

With these changes happening, you have to move fast enough to keep up. Your doing so will help you gain brand recognition and popularity in various social media platforms. Get out there and start learning, testing and watching others do their thing. Then, immediately apply.

About the Author

Gary Vaynerchuk is an American-Belarusian storytelling entrepreneur. In 1998, he graduated from college and took over the daily operations of his father's liquor store in Springfield, New Jersey. He renamed it to Wine Library and delved into selling their products online. In 2006, he started a daily webcast on wine known as Wine Library TV.

With his strategy in e-commerce, pricing, and marketing, by 2005, he was able to grow the business from $3 million to $60 million of annual revenue. In 2011, he stepped away from managing Wine Library and started VaynerMedia, a digital advertising agency, with his brother.

VaynerMedia works with companies included in the Fortune 500. It helps these companies develop strategies in digital and social media marketing and content production.

He was selected by Businessweek as one of the top twenty entrepreneurs people should follow and as one of the top 25 tech investors by CNN.

He lives in New York City and is an avid fan of the New York Jets, a football team that he aims to own someday.

Conclusion

From this book, you have learned the new reality of marketing your brand and business to your target customers. Marketing by constant interruption with tempting offers is a thing of the past. The new norm is providing valuable content that will build the relationship with your customers. When you've built this relationship, it will be the time when you pitch in your offer to your customer. Refusal to acknowledge this reality will cause your marketing efforts to stagnate and to remain in the pre-social media age.

You can use the tips here to develop quality content so that you can translate into the native content of a social media platform. With these pointers, you can create content that does not interrupt your audience's social media experience, piques their interest, provides value, reveals the character of your brand, and adapts according to your audience's preference.

Then, you were taught the native content for the current popular platforms of social media. Facebook gives importance to content found valuable by its users. Twitter values well-received, popular, and timely content that were spun from either internal or external sources. Pinterest places priority on images that users find interesting or inspiring. Instagram and its community like aesthetically attractive images. Tumblr likes content spun from original or repurposed images that catches the users' interest. By knowing the content native to these platforms, you can function more effectively in catching attention and conveying your story to your audience. Of course, ranking of content isn't done manually by people, so some technical information on ranking algorithms was given so you can adapt accordingly.

With how changes can happen as regards to how platforms work, as well as the introduction of new ones, some platforms were reviewed to teach you how to spot opportunities in platforms not covered in the book. Some platforms that have potential in the future were also discussed. By utilizing and learning how these platforms work, you can gain experience and knowledge on how to assess social media platforms in the future. Therefore, in the future, you can have a greater potential in creating your own success in a platform not covered in the book.

Gary explained the most important factor in creating the success that you're seeking with social media marketing. He stated that effort is the greatest equalizer amidst disadvantages in technical ability and financial resources. He further indicated that sincere interactions and genuine care towards your audience is the key in getting an advantage over your bigger competitors.

By applying the concepts taught to you, you can achieve significant advantage by increasing brand awareness through effective social media marketing. This is where people spend most of their time now, and this makes it the perfect place, at the moment, to build relationships with potential consumers. Obviously, you will have to learn and apply these concepts to gain the benefits they offer. If you wholly learn the intricacies of social media, you can even gain significant advantage over those who know less than you do.

Of course, like any strategy, the concepts in this book will not last forever. There will be a need to adapt, to learn, and, again, to adapt. If there's one thing the social media age has taught us is that things can change dramatically. It could become a totally new thing, which can be seen with what happened in marketing due to social media. Nevertheless, by constantly adapting your strategies and business to the current age, this should not be a bother and it could even serve as a great mindset in the pursuit of competitive advantage. If you learn how to adapt with the inevitable changes in technology, there's no stopping you from succeeding even in the midst of these changes.

Final Thoughts

Hey! Did you enjoy this book? We sincerely hope you thoroughly enjoyed this short read and have gotten immensely valuable insights that will help you in any areas of your life.

Would it be too greedy if we ask for a review from you?

It takes 1 minute to leave 1 review to possibly influence 1 more person's decision to read just 1 book which may change their 1 life. Your 1 minute matters and we value it and thank you so much for giving us your 1 minute. If it sucks, just say it sucks. Period.

FREE BONUS

<u>P.S. Is it okay if we overdeliver?</u>

Here at Abbey Beathan Publishing, we believe in overdelivering way beyond our reader's expectations. Is it okay if we overdeliver?

Here's the deal, we're going to give you an extremely valuable cheatsheet of "Accelerated Learning". We've partnered up with Ikigai Publishing to present to you the exclusive bonus of "Accelerated Learning Cheatsheet"

What's the catch? We need to trust you… You see, we want to overdeliver and in order for us to do that, we've to trust our reader to keep this bonus a secret to themselves. Why? Because we don't want people to be getting our exclusive accelerated learning cheatsheet without even buying our books itself. Unethical, right?

Ok. Are you ready?

Simply Visit this link: http://bit.ly/acceleratedcheatsheet

We hope you'll enjoy our free bonuses as much as we've enjoyed preparing it for you!

Free Bonus #2: Free Book Preview of Summary: God: A Human History

The Book at a Glance

God: A Human History is a journey through the history of mankind's attempt to know God from ancient times to the advent of Islam. Just like in Genesis, the book begins at the beginning of time but it presents the story from a scientific perspective. It then follows Adam and Eve's progress as hunter-gatherers to farmers and finally to civilization builders, describing the changes that occurred within their minds and in their societies as their belief in God evolved. At the very end, it reveals a startling secret that is a product of Reza Asians' religious scholarship and personal search for the truth of what God is.

Part One: The Embodied Soul

Chapter 1: Adam and Eve in Eden

The first chapter applies the creation story to what science has found so far and describes what could be the very root of the invention of religion – the soul.

Chapter 2: The Lord of the Beasts

The Lord of the Beasts narrates how prehistoric people viewed divinity as someone who is similar to themselves but with power over nature.

Chapter 3: The Face in the Tree

The Face in the Tree further explains the ancient notion of the embodiment of the soul by describing the instinctive compulsion to see humanity in nature.

Part Two: The Humanized God

Chapter 4: Spears into Plows

Having discovered agriculture, humans experienced changes in their worldview and the gods changed along with it.

Chapter 5: Lofty Persons

The idea of gods as lofty persons became more prominent and this idea spread through different lands, producing various gods.

Chapter 6: The High God

There have been times in history when some people claimed a god was the only god there was; this chapter tells the story of humanity's first attempts at monotheism.

Part Three: What is God?

Chapter 7: God is One

Moses came to know a God who proclaimed that He is the only one there is, and this time, the goal to worship a singular god became successful

Chapter 8: God is Three

Jesus' arrival as described in the New Testament implied a predicament to the notion that God is a singular god, thus, Church leaders sought a way to explain that God is three in one.

Chapter 9: God is All

From the deserts of Arabia comes Islam, and unlike Christianity, its god is one without a human image.

Introduction: In Our Image

As a child, Reza Aslan imagined that God was like his father, but larger, and had magical powers. He saw him sitting in a throne among the clouds – his voice boomed when he was angry, but he could also laugh and cry. He wasn't sure where he got this description, whether he had glimpsed it in a painting, learned in a storybook, or he was simply born with the notion. Despite this, he acknowledged that according to research, people usually think about God as a human with supernatural abilities.

He grew up fascinated by spirituality and religion, wanting to know what God is really like. He wanted to feel the presence of God in his life, but he perceived a great gap between him and the deity. When he was a teen, he left Islam and became Christian like his friends. His new religion gave him hope that he could finally bridge the chasm simply by imagining God as an absolutely perfect human being.

Eventually, this limited conception of God disappointed him and he gave up Christianity and came back to Islam. He had found a new attraction to this religion because it teaches that God cannot be defined by images whether they are human-like or not. On the other hand, he noticed that Muslims cannot help but think of their God in human terms, and they ascribe human vices and virtues, flaws and feelings to it just like others.

He discovered that humanizing the divine is hardwired in the brain, thus it is common in almost all religions. This tendency to bestow human virtues, vices, and even bodies to God stemmed from the need to comprehend the divine, and it reflects in all religions.

Aslan is not claiming that a God doesn't exist and that it's just an invention of humans. For him, there is no proof of both the existence and absence of God. He says that faith, or deciding to believe in something that's beyond the natural world exists, is a choice.

Religion is a language of metaphors and symbols that provides a way for believers to communicate the inexpressible. Throughout religions' history, in almost all of the religions of the world, the greatest metaphor for God is none other than the human being. We bestow on God not only the good qualities such as our ability to show compassion and seek justice, but also the vile things like our greed, aggression, bigotry, bias, and violence.

The consequence of humanizing the divine is to divinize human attributes. God's desires are ours, but without our human limitations, and we convince ourselves that these wishes belong to God. God's actions are based on what we do, but without negative consequences.

This explains why throughout history, religion has led to good and evil deeds, and why two individuals can read the same scriptures and yet still have opposing interpretations.

Aslan realizes that the notion of God he was seeking for was too broad to be confined by any single religious tradition, and experiencing divinity requires dehumanizing God in his consciousness.

Thus, the book is not just a history of how humans have humanized God, it is also a plea to stop ascribing human compulsions to the divine, and instead develop a pantheistic view towards God. This may be done by remembering that we humans have fashioned our God in our image.

Read More...

CPSIA information can be obtained
at www.ICGtesting.com
Printed in the USA
BVHW081936210819
556437BV00001B/58/P